I0211024

Relict

poems by

Brian Mosher

Finishing Line Press
Georgetown, Kentucky

Relict

ACKNOWLEDGMENTS

The author is also grateful to the editors of the following publications for publishing previous versions of some of these poems:

"No Small Hole" (an early version of "My Uncles, My Father and Me"), *Written Tales*
"Nevertheless," *Alien Buddha* 'Zine #57
"Too Late," Oddball Magazine
"Dr. O'Little," *Coneflower Cafe* from Choeofpleirn Press
"I Remember the Blood Mostly," *Sink Hole*
"Crossing Generations," which has since become the poems, "Backdrop" and "Uncle Ed's Stove," *Rituals* from Anomaly Poetry
"Lost in the Fall," *eMerge*
"My Great Grandfather's Horse," *Tidings*, from Anomaly Poetry
"The Final Decision," *eMerge*

Publisher: Leah Huete de Maines
Editor: Christen Kincaid
Interior Photos: Brian Mosher
Cover Art: Kevin C. Myron
Author Photo: Courtney C. Pugliese
Cover Design: Elizabeth Maines McCleavy

Order online: www.finishinglinepress.com
also available on amazon.com

Author inquiries and mail orders:
Finishing Line Press
PO Box 1626
Georgetown, Kentucky 40324
USA

Contents

My parents, Betty and Ray Mosher, circa 1955

My father, Raymond Mosher Korea 1955

My father Ray and his brothers, Bruce, Herb and Don. Best of friends for a lifetime.

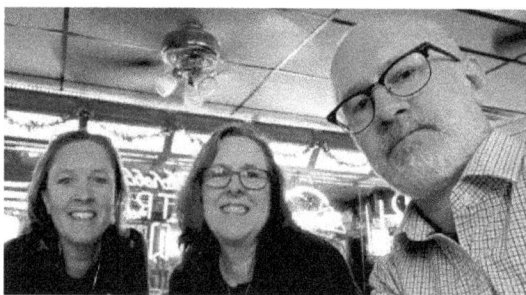

My sisters, Janet and Stephanie, and myself.

*Dedicated to the memory of my father,
Raymond Mosher, 1931-2018, the best of men;
and with gratitude to my siblings, Stephanie Walsh and Janet Orde.*

Part I

Bye for now

"Bye for now," he'd say
on parting, every time.
Not the fragmentary "bye"
nor the too-final-sounding "good-bye."
Always, "bye for now."

Backdrop

In a photograph, four brothers,
youngest to oldest, left to right:
my father and uncles,
who all share my face.
Next, their father and his,
named for the genocidal Andrew Jackson.

I let myself imagine
this naming gives some insight
into the minds and hearts
of the generation before.
But the truer insight comes
from having known the younger men,
the gentlest men I've known,

None of whom ever lived more
than twenty miles from the house
which forms the backdrop of this photo,
of their lives.

My Great-Grandfather's Horse

He was working over in Mansfield,
and his wife was home alone
when one of the cows got sick,
or choked on an apple or something.

She hitched the old horse to the wagon,
drove over to where her husband was, full speed.
By the time she arrived, the poor old horse
was sweaty and breathless. She told him,
'The cow is in trouble,' and he said,
'Well, that's no reason to kill the horse.'

Remembering a Housefire, 1940

"A hot day to begin with,
the fire and smoke just made it hotter."
They tell me, and it's as if I'm there,
one of the kids from the neighborhood
who climb into the back of
their dad's old dump truck.
The Henderson place is on fire
and we go to watch the firemen
try to save it.

"Old Man Henderson was burning
brush and leaves right next to the house.
Next thing he knows the whole place is in flames."

"The fire spread quickly, too,
through the woods down there, toward
Ed Landry's place.
Ed lost some shingles to the crackling embers."

"Old Man Henderson claimed he had permission
from the fire department to burn brush,
but there was talk afterward
he didn't have any permit."

They all laugh silently together,
these three old men,
the flames of a fire from eighty years ago dancing
in their suddenly childish eyes.

He Was Born

My father was born
during the depression, but
you never met a less
depressed person,
"could be worse"
among his most used phrases
in the face of any crisis.

Born to brotherhood,
closer than any siblings I know,
with weekly meetings at the homestead
exchanging news, recalling the past.

Born to work,
to herd chickens and gather eggs,
operate drill presses,
drive the van full of his ladies,
senior citizens,
as if he were not one himself.

Not born to scholarship or study,
dropped out of school
(a lifelong regret),
relied instead on natural wisdom,
inherent knowledge,
as a river knows where to flow,
as the oak tree understands
the value of its shadow.

Not a fighter,
such a gentle man,
yet found himself a soldier,
crossing the "frozen Chosin"
with no choice but to fight
and, thankfully, survive.

I don't believe he ever fought again.

Born to faith,
believed in the goodness of people,
all people, and in second chances,
and seventh chances,
and seventy times seven chances,
and forgiveness and love.

Uncle Ed's Stove

I came to know my mother's ancestors
through the sourness of a crisp, green apple
picked from the tree in Uncle Ed's yard.

Every Granny Smith since
takes me back to Aunt Gus
telling stories
over cups of tea beside the
wood-stove which heated that house,
cooked meals
for one hundred and fifty years,
dried snow-wet socks and burned yesterday's news,
on which she cooked for us
peas and beans and
new potatoes,
I hated at the time.

That stove, fueled by branches and logs
cut from the forest outside the back door,
provided generations
with heat and comfort,
until Ed and Gus's son
built a new modern split-level on the site
(complete with rumpus room and pool table),
after having the old homestead
towed down the road, stove and all.

But they saved the apple tree,
so I can still believe.

My Mother's Red Hair

My mother's red hair,
she was told, condemned her:
short-tempered, consequences be damned.
But she gripped my sister's arm
in a fit of rage one afternoon
over a transgression no one
today remembers, with an anger which
cannot be blamed on the hue of hair.

No, hers was a rage born of fear,
born the day her mother died.
A twelve-year-old motherless
child learned to cling to what she could.

She clung to us all with those grasping
hands as a shipwrecked castaway
to a piece of flotsam,
leaving fingerprints on our memories
to match those on my sister's flesh.

At times it seemed she'd drown us all,
dragging us down to lightless depths,
until her thinning hair faded
to white and the strength in her
arms failed her,
leaving us to do the holding.

Measure

Today, as I shed selfish tears, the child
who lives within me sees my loss refracted
by the prism of my father's tears
on the day of the first death I knew,
when he had to give Mom the news
her father's heart had finally failed.

Silently, he held her, his shoulders shaking,
as she howled her pain against his chest.
Quiet tears of empathy filled his eyes,
this the only time I ever saw him cry.
Such was the measure of this man,
the loss which hurt him most was not his own.

My Uncles, My Father, and Me

We sit in a circle of green plastic lawn chairs
in what Don, my youngest uncle, calls,
"The meeting that never ends."

Red-faced with the humiliation of divorce,
I feel a child among these men
for whom vows are always kept,
and bear witness to their quiet ritual
beneath an ancient maple.

They recall long since chopped down apple trees,
a hammock hung between;
berries which grew wild here
in what Ray, my father, calls, "the war years,"
as if there ever were a year without a war.
He reminds me, "This was the big war. Everything
was different. Ford even stopped making cars."

And the house, this house of their lives,
built by hand, the foundation hole dug
with a horse and a wooden scoop,
blood and sweat in every board and nail.

I feel connected to them,
through them, yet,
it is a slender thread.
As they each leave this life,
the thread grows thinner.

I recall all this years later,
now the family's oldest living man,
a lesser man among the ghosts of greater.

Part II

I Remember the Blood, Mostly

I know, objectively, it wasn't much,
but it seemed a flood, dark red,
smooth at first, as it pooled beneath his head,
then frothing, bubbling.

Face down on the hardwood,
halfway out of the bathroom,
his breath pushed the blood,
spread it wider, toward the linen closet.

Then all was still.

 Death hovered.

A voice on the phone said,
"Turn him over"—I turned him.
"Clear his airway"—my fingers did what I did not know they could.
"Breathe in his mouth twice"—I breathed.
"Press on his chest"—I pressed.
I pressed again.
He breathed, coughed, spit.

Police, EMTs, firemen appeared,
took control, told me I had saved him.

But saved for what? Delivered into what?
Tubes, wires, straps, stitches, surgeries.
Ten days in a twilight
before death finally claimed him,
completing the process
I had only interrupted.

I washed the floor later.
I washed the towels the rescuers
had pulled from the linen closet.
No signs remain. But these years later, I still see. And taste.

Dr. O'Little

One thing I don't remember is the name of the
diminutive Irish doctor at Rhode Island Hospital,
with his red hair, freckles and charming brogue.

He told us right away there was little cause for hope.
But he seemed so young,
what could he tell us of hope?

And so, we let them intubate and ventilate,
not knowing how to give up on this most hopeful of men,
and not being prepared to say good-bye.

Ten days later, still unprepared,
we said good-bye after he was already gone.

Regret? Of course, some days.
But how were we to know on that first day,

amid the panic and the fear:
tiny Dr. O'Little was wiser than he appeared.

Lost in the Fall

Just days after the fall,
in a hospital ward
rendered hopeless
by wires and tubes
and the ineffectual odor of disinfectant,
angry fire flashed in his eyes,
finger pointed accusingly—
a first between my father and me,
despite ample opportunities:
> my failure to finish college, tuition money squandered;
> jobs lost to incompetence, or worse, to dishonesty;
> a marriage ended in disaster, for much the same reasons.

No longer the man I knew
since the night he crashed
to the hardwood floor
after a 2 a.m. piss,
he wanted now only
to take a shit on a toilet like a man,
not in a diaper like a child,
and he saw me there, not helping,
only saying, "They'll be here soon."

Mercifully, nurses rescued him from his need,
but not me from my shame.
Nor could they prevent this
from becoming part of how I still see him,
and of how I judge myself.

The Final Decision

His doctor's call raised us
from not-quite sleep,
"Come now
if you want to say
good bye."

Ever he had carried us
on slender shoulders—
taxi-driver or batting practice pitcher—
no matter how tired
from a day at the factory.

And now, as when we were children,
tucking us in warm and clean
before putting himself to bed,
he had waited until we were
safely out of sight,
before letting go of life.

A Heat Less Durable

The request surprises me:
"Would you help us close the casket?"
I imagine he means we'll lower
the lid by hand, as a suitcase or a hope chest.

Attaching a small crank
to the exterior, below the hinge,
inches from my father's waxy corpse,
he explains the procedure:
"Just turn this clockwise."

It seems impossible,
this unexpected, undesired task,
but the lid does close as I turn the crank,
unaware of the still stealthy virus
which had invaded during the preceding
sleepless days and nights
of watching my father die.

Next morning, gathered around
the freshly opened grave,
we mix our mourning with the falling sleet
in the ceremonial final moment.

As if the slow turning of the crank,
had not been final enough.

Later, surrounded by loved ones
for sandwiches and coffee, I feel a heat
more immediate than grief.

For three days I hide in the dark,
sweating and shivering,
until the infection wears itself out,
leaves me alone with the other invader,
whose work is not yet complete.

Lighter Than Any Feather

He would not have known the name Anubis,
but his heart, as light as any feather,
would surely have passed the test,
been allowed to cross.

He was not familiar with
the legend of the river Styx,
but with or without a piece of silver,
the ferryman could not have refused him passage.

You'll say I'm blinded to his faults.
You'll say I refuse to see his sins.
You may be right, it matters not.
Not for me the task of judgement.

I cannot read the book of life
written in my father's soul.
I know only what I know.

The Things He Left Me

From my father I inherited
this long face, this thin-limbed body,
thinning hair, and undersized bladder.

We share an underestimation
of our own self-worth,
stemming from (or leading to)
not graduating public school (him),
dropping out of college (me).

But I have not his impulse to channel
that lack into a life of service,
carrying his passengers' groceries
to their door, and devoting years
of his widowerhood to a new lady
with her crippling illness and poverty,
while I spend my divorced years
hiding from any social responsibility.

He gave me his weak back and scrawny arms,
but not the fortitude and work ethic
to shovel and rake despite them.

I retained his desire for closeness with siblings,
but not his comfort with
the unannounced pop-in visit.

And while I may have received some
fraction of his unerring morality,
and awareness of wrong and right,
this awareness did not prevent me
from repeated late nights out, my wife
and child waiting and worrying at home.

Perhaps this trait skipped a generation,
for I see my daughter walk in his morally
upright shoes, as a teacher of things neither he or I ever learned.

*My neighborhood-nosiness and this bunion must have come
from my mother.

Too Late

In life we wrote no letters.
So close, why would we bother?
But the chasm of death lies between us now,
and I write to fill the gap.

I heard your voice as I set out today:
"it's time to get an oil change."
Thanks for that, you know I tend to forget
so many of those necessary tasks.

The thought of oil reminds me of sitting
in your lap in your fake-leather chair,
combing your thinning hair, its greasy scent
still with me, even as my own hair disappears.

Which reminds me of the odor and sounds of the
model train we set up in the only room with empty space.
Who needs a bathroom that size?
It was bigger than any of our bedrooms.

The real reason I'm writing is to ask your advice:
I can't get this garbage disposal to work.
You know I'm no good with gadgets.
Please respond if you can.

Also, send along your chug-chugging laugh, I'm
beginning to run out of the supply I'd stored up,
And I miss the feeling of my hand crushed in yours.
No one shakes like that anymore.

I don't expect a reply.
That's not how the world works.
This is just my way of not forgetting
the feeling of riding on your shoulders.

Part III

Scorekeeper

You tied a rope around the neck
of all the promises I broke.

You never swayed,
you never rocked,

You only rolled
onto your other side.

Whatever we had, I know
you believe I threw it away,

and you're the one
who always kept score, so,

I'm sure you know
I'm the one to blame.

A Tangled Web

The truth: I needed time alone between
the office drudgery and responsibilities
of home. The lie: "Traffic was so
much heavier than usual."
I spent the difference at the bar
drinking my way vainly toward clarity.

>Behind a tapestry of lies, a curtain of
>intertwining falsehoods, I hid my private
>joys and fears, hoping they would
>remain my own, unshared, undiluted by
>the opinions and criticisms of others.

The truth: I craved a sexual intimacy
which she did not. The lie: "It doesn't
matter, we can find intimacy
in other forms of closeness."
I spent the difference purchasing the
illusion of what I craved from strangers.

>Mesmerized by the intricacy of the strands,
>the artistry of the emerging patterns,
>I blinded myself to the pain of those
>I had promised to care about the most,
>those who deserved at least my honesty.

The truth: I squandered our
savings on these empty vanities.
The lie: "You wasted our
money on things we don't need."
I spent the difference ignoring the fact
she was only filling her own emptiness.

When my shroud of deceit unraveled
beneath the weight of its own complexity,
I paid the price for my duplicity:
humiliation, isolation, poverty, shame,
alone; perhaps, my intention all along.

And when the lie was, "I don't know
why," the truth was I knew no other
way to express my self-loathing than
by destroying what I knew
I did not deserve.

Nevertheless

It's true, I do believe
the world revolves around me.
There is no other way it can be.
Admit it, it's the same for you.
Wherever I plant my feet,
wherever I sit my ass,
there is the center of all mass
in the universe,
the one unmoving place.
I am my own axis mundi.

Yet, there is another still-point
around which the universe spins.
I know, I know, the physics don't work.
Nevertheless:
The Common, as the townies call it,
the symbolic center of my youth,
remains an almost timeless patch
of green surrounded by asphalt,
a quaint, quiet place amidst
the traffic and the commerce.

I don't love everything about the town.
I don't love the jingoistic super-patriotism,
or the link to those other Patriots™.
I don't love the inability to let go
of the outmoded name of the school
sports teams. But I love The Common,
and feel its pull each time I am in town.
"Like touching home in a game of tag,"
I tell my sister, who laughs at this sentimentality
from her older, cynical brother.
Nevertheless.

Return To the Scene

Like images in a mirror,
my uncle's death resembles my father's
as one oak tree does the next,
as their faces did each other,
as mine resembles them both.

The same ward, same suite of rooms
where I held my father's hand
to comfort myself, now holds my uncle,
his lifelong best friend and almost-twin,
who reaches his hand to me.

Beeping monitors, the hum of machinery,
the compressing thump of ventilators,
rubber wheeled meal-carts
squeaking across linoleum,
hushed voices, muffled moans;

compassionate nurses and
emotionless doctors,
the worried faces of loved-ones
repeated in room after room along a
disorienting maze of identical hallways;

amid the acrid acid smell of urine-soaked sheets,
of impotent antiseptic, of illness and decay,
time collapses, disappears,
folds back on itself, or forward,
and I do not know whose bedside I sit at,
whose death I dread.

Just as…

Just as a shadow drags itself
across the hardwood floor
at 4 AM on a moonless
Sunday night

Just as the neighbor's dogs do
their best hyena imitations
and the branch of an old oak
tree scrapes the window screen

Just as the hum of the refrigerator
drones in a heartbeat rhythm
but fails to outshout the never
ending monologue in my head

Just as the furnace roars into
life in the basement below,
and the occasional car splashes
by on the snow-wet road outside

I am still parentless,
and sleepless, but not yet hopeless,
as the rhythms of life
continue to carry me forward.

The Same Hands

after John Keats' "This living hand..."

These hands which held my daughter still fresh from the womb,
stroked her hair before she had completed her escape,
then diapered and bathed and powdered and clothed her
until she, with her own hands, took her own direction,
these hands I look at now and do not recognize.

When did these spots appear?
   One of many echoes of the father.
When did the knuckles begin to swell?
   The mother is here, as well.
Cracks and wrinkles and lines defy recollection.

These still living hands
contain no memories,
only echoes and scars,
only aches and clicks.

Though they turned the crank to close
my father's coffin, sealing his waxy face away
from us who still had need of him—the final
symbolic end to a life well-lived—yet,
these icy hands have hope to mingle with
the scars, to soothe the aches, to warm
the joints, as I watch that baby, now a woman,
forge her own life of love and commitment.

With Thanks

Thank you to Wayne-Daniel Berard, Sarah Letourneau, Miriam O'Neal, Paul Szlosek, Ron Whittle, Robert Eugene Perry, Sarah Jane Ferreira and all the other hosts and facilitators of readings and open mic venues. You're keeping the flame alive and I'm grateful for the opportunity to have warmed myself.

Thank you to Eileen Cleary, whose chapbook workshop was instrumental in helping these poems find their current shape.

Thank you to John L. Holgerson, Mark Walsh, and Elizabeth Birch, aka the Uncommon, for the invaluable feedback on many of these poems in our monthly sessions, and for the friendship.

Brian Mosher cannot remember a time when he didn't write. Beginning with fictional "biographies" of friends in High School, to Bob Dylan-inspired song lyrics during what should have been college years, to music reviews for multiple underground publications in the early 2000s, writing has always been part of how he identifies himself and how he examines the world around him.

Having self-published three collections of poetry and prose between 2016 and 2021, his first professionally published chapbook was *Dreams and Other Magic* (Alien Buddha Press 2023), which explores the unconscious world of dreams and fantasies. In 2025, Metaphysical Fox Press published a full-length collection of poems and song lyrics titled *A Muster of Melodious Musings*, containing work written primarily between 2016-2024. His poems and short stories have appeared in multiple journals and magazines, including *Blue Villa, Nixes Mate, eMerge, Books and Pieces, Confetti, Rituals, Coneflower Cafe, Written Tales, Esoterica Magazine,* and *Half and One Magazine.*

Mosher is a native of southeastern Massachusetts, spending his childhood in the town known for it's professional football franchise. He preferred them in the 1970s when they weren't very good, but it was easy to get tickets.

His favorite ways to pass time are reading and listening to music, and he draws inspiration for much of his writing from observations made from barstools. He also frequents many open mic and poetry reading venues throughout the area.

www.ingramcontent.com/pod-product-compliance
Lightning Source LLC
Chambersburg PA
CBHW022045080426
42734CB00009B/1245